YOUR FAITH
In God Will Work

Kenneth E. Hagin

Chapter 1
YOUR FAITH IN GOD WILL WORK

Through faith we understand that the worlds were framed by the word of God, so that things which are seen were not made of things which do appear.

— Hebrews 11:3

When you know this verse, you know the "why" of faith.

The Bible says in Genesis 1:1, *"In the beginning God created. . . ."*

How did He create? Our text says the worlds were created by the *Word* of God. He created them by the word of faith.

He said, *". . . Let there be . . . ,"* and there *was*!

God had faith that His own words would come to pass.

We know from the Scripture that Jesus had faith in His own words too.

MARK 11:12-14; 20-22

12 . . . when they were come from Bethany, he [Jesus] was hungry:

13 And seeing a fig tree afar off having leaves, he came, if haply he might find anything thereon: and when he came to it, he found nothing but leaves; for the time of figs was not yet.

14 And Jesus answered and said unto it, No man eat fruit of thee hereafter for ever. And his disciples heard it. . . .

20 And in the morning, as they passed by, they saw the fig tree dried up from the roots.

21 And Peter calling to remembrance saith

Chapter 3
HOW YOU CAN OVERCOME THE DEVIL

And having spoiled principalities and powers, he made a shew of them openly, triumphing over them in it.

— Colossians 2:15

The Bible teaches us here that Jesus put Satan to nought and He triumphed over him. Another translation reads, "He stripped him." What did He strip Satan of? His authority over man.

When Jesus put Satan to nought and stripped him of his authority, it was you in Christ who did that work. Christ acted in your stead — in your place. He did it for you.

1 JOHN 4:4
4 Ye are of God, little children, and have overcome them: because greater is he that is in you, than he that is in the world.

Who is the "them" we have overcome? We find from reading the first three verses of First John chapter 4 that John was talk-

whether he knows it or not. (If he doesn't know it, he can't walk in the light of it — but it's still his.)

This redemption is personal. It is an absolute redemption from the dominion of the devil.

Satan does not have dominion over us any longer.

Satan is not our Lord or our Master. Jesus is.

Satan has no right to rule us with sin, sickness, or anything else that belongs to him.

This redemption belongs to every believer. It's my personal property and your personal property.

To increase your faith, repeat out loud: "It is *my* personal property. It is *my* redemption. It belongs to *me*."

You see, Christ was our Substitute. He took our place. (That truth often falls on deaf ears because that's not the way we have been taught; nevertheless, we still need to grasp it.)

translated "justified" can also be translated "made righteous.") Jesus didn't die
for my trespasses any more than He died
for your trespasses. It's ours, glory to God!

COLOSSIANS 1:13,14
**13 Who hath delivered us from the power of
darkness, and hath translated us into the
kingdom of his dear Son:
14 In whom we have redemption through his
blood, even the forgiveness of sins.**

The Christian, then, can confidently
say, "He delivered us," or to make it personal, "He delivered me."

The individual Christian can confidently say, "He delivered me out of the
power (or authority) of darkness." The
Greek word translated "power" here is
translated "authority" elsewhere in the
King James New Testament. So we could
say, "God delivered me out of the *authority*
of darkness and has translated me into the
Kingdom of his dear Son."

Friends, this does not belong to just a
few. This absolute redemption is the personal property of *every* child of God,

more than they do. Yes, somebody else may have more light, and they're walking in that light, but everyone born into the family of God enjoys the same redemption.

The child of God has been redeemed out of the hand of the enemy. Every one of us has. *Satan was conquered for you personally.* Satan was conquered for me personally. (When I say it like that, it buoys up my faith.)

The believer can say, along with the Apostle Paul, ". . . [Jesus] *was delivered for our offences, and was raised again for our justification*" (Rom. 4:25). A translation I like better reads, "He was delivered up on account of our trespasses, and He was raised for our justification."

It's ours — mine and yours! It belongs to us, so I can make that personal. I can say He was delivered on account of *my* offenses, and He was raised for *my* justification.

Redemption belongs to every one of us. Furthermore, I'm not any more justified than you are, and you're not any more justified than I am. (The same Greek word

6

thing against themselves: their unworthiness, their unfitness, their weakness, their lack of faith, etc.

If we can get these people to let us pray and believe for them, we can get answers for them — temporarily. But Satan will rob them of the blessings God intended for them to have unless we teach them the facts of God's Word (not what we *think* about it; not how we've got it *figured out*; but what the Bible *actually says*).

A Bible fact that gave me faith was this: *God, my Heavenly Father, does not have any favorite children.* He loves every one of us with the same love.

Sometimes natural parents have a favorite child — we've seen that — but God doesn't have any favorites. Get that fact down in your spirit by saying out loud, "God has no favorites."

Every person born into the family of God has the same redemption. You are not any more saved than I am, and I am not any more saved than you are.

Somehow in people's faulty thinking they assume that another Christian has

Chapter 2
GOD HAS NO FAVORITES

Why don't some people believe that their faith in God will work? I know from experience that a lot of people have faith in *my* faith and the faith of others. But they do not have confidence that their own faith in God will work. For some reason, they do not believe in themselves. They do not believe in what Christ has wrought for them. They do not believe who and what they are in Christ Jesus.

The reason for their unbelief is that they do not know what the Bible teaches about who they are in the Lord Jesus Christ. They need to find out.

They have a feeling they are not good enough.

They feel their faith is not strong enough.

They're acquainted with all of their own failings and weaknesses, and they readily accept every bit of condemnation they hear preached to them from the pulpit.

They are always willing to believe any-

shall not doubt in his heart, but shall
BELIEVE that those things which he SAITH
shall come to pass; he shall have whatsoever
he SAITH.

Things that you *say* are words.

Notice two more things about verse 23:
(1) He believes in his *heart*; (2) He believes
that what he says will come to pass.
Another way to say it is like this: He
believes that his own faith in God will
work.

Did you ever stop to think about it?
Evidently God had faith in His own words
because He spoke words of faith and they
came to pass. Evidently Jesus had faith in
His own words, because He spoke to the fig
tree, and what He said came to pass.

And when we speak God's Word out of
our mouths, we can have confidence that it
will come to pass for us. In other words,
our own faith in God will work.

unto him, Master, behold, the fig tree which
thou cursedst is withered away.
22 And Jesus answering saith unto them,
Have faith in God.

Notice Jesus said, ". . . *Have faith in
God.*" The literal meaning of that phrase is
"have the faith of God." Jesus used the fig
tree to demonstrate that He had that God-
kind of faith. Then He said to the
disciples — and to us — "*You,* have that
kind of faith."

He went on to say in the next verse
"*For . . . whosoever shall say . . . and shall
not doubt in his heart, but shall believe
that those things which he saith shall come
to pass; he shall have whatsoever he saith*"
(Mark 11:23).

Jesus operated in the God-kind of faith.
He encouraged His disciples to exercise
that kind of faith. And He said that
"whosoever" could operate in it.

MARK 11:23
23 For verily I say unto you, That *WHOSO-
EVER* shall SAY unto this mountain, Be thou
removed, and be thou cast into the sea; and

Chapter 5
WHO ARE YOU?

In the natural realm, our children partake of our nature. We hear people say, "He acts just like his daddy. He looks just like his daddy." Well, that's because he's got his daddy's nature in the flesh.

I can remember when Ken was in Bible college. He'd go out on weekends to preach, sometimes with a group of students and sometimes on his own. He did a lot of his preaching in East Texas. I had preached in virtually every Full Gospel church of any size there, and I also had pastored in that area.

People said to Ken, "You sound just like your daddy."

Well, he tried to change, but when he tried to be something he wasn't, he'd become self-conscious and lose the anointing. He tried to preach something else besides faith, yet faith was burning in him, because he'd heard it all his life.

He came to me and told me his problem.

I said, "Well, don't let that bother you. Naturally you would sound like me. You are my son. I'd sure hate for you to look and sound like some other man! That would be quite embarrassing."

I said, "When they say, 'You sound just like your daddy,' you say, 'Bless God, he's my daddy. I ought to sound like him.'"

That released him. After our talk, he threw caution to the wind, went ahead and preached faith, and got back his anointing.

When our children, Ken and Pat, were small, it was very difficult when we had to reprimand or correct them, which parents have to do sometimes. Parents will understand *why* it was difficult: You see yourself in your children. (You single folks don't know what we are talking about. You'll learn, though.)

Friends, spiritually speaking, you are born of God. You've got God's nature. The life of God is in your spirit. You are His child. He's your father. You can say, "He has declared me righteous. He has made me righteous. I am the righteousness of God in Christ."

Make this confession out loud: "I am the righteousness of God in Christ."

Shut your eyes and say it. Listen to your voice say it again and again.

I get quite amused at Christian people sometimes. Some don't know who they are. You could understand that kind of a spirit in somebody who doesn't know Christ and is searching for reality. Naturally *they* don't know who they are or where they're going. But for a Christian not to know who he or she is, is amusing!

I know who I am!

I'm a new creature in Christ Jesus.

I'm a child of God.

I'm an heir of God.

I'm a joint-heir with Jesus Christ.

I'm the righteousness of God. Hallelujah!

Chapter 6
THE NAME OF JESUS AND YOU

Here's another Bible fact: *The Name of Jesus belongs to every believer, every child of God.*

That Name doesn't belong to just a few any more than *Jesus* belongs to just a few. We have a right to the Name of Jesus. No one has a better right to the use of the Name of Jesus than you!

I want you to say that out loud: "No one has a better right to the Name of Jesus than I do."

Believe it when you say it.

You see, all authority is in that Name. You can say, "Jesus declares that whatever I ask in His Name, He will give it to me. So I take my place fearlessly. I lay my hands upon loved ones who are sick and say, 'In the Name of Jesus, disease leave this body. And don't you ever touch this loved one again!" Praise God, you've got a right to do that. The Name of Jesus belongs to you.

Christ said, and you can say, too, "... *these signs shall follow them that believe; In my* [Jesus'] *name shall they cast out devils . . . they shall lay hands on the sick, and they shall recover"* (Mark 16:17,18).

To whom is Jesus talking? He's talking to *believers*: These signs shall follow them that believe. I accept it at face value and I act upon it, because He said it to me and to you too.

To get this truth down into your spirit, repeat this confession out loud:

"He said it to me.

"The Name of Jesus belongs to me.

"In the Name of Jesus, I lay hands on the sick, and they shall recover.

"The Name of Jesus belongs to me personally.

"The Name of Jesus is the personal property of every believer.

"No one has a better right to use that Name than I do.

"The Name of Jesus belongs to me.

"All authority in Heaven and on earth is wrapped up in that Name.

"And that Name belongs to me."

At the close of our Prayer and Healing

School service every afternoon, we used to sing, "Keep the Switch of Faith Turned On." What does it mean, "Keep the switch of faith turned on"? The Bible says, *". . . they shall lay hands on the sick, and they shall recover"* (Mark 16:18). Once hands are laid on you for healing, start believing — no matter what may *seem* to be: "The healing power of God is ministered to me. It's working in me, and I shall recover."

I was pastoring once in a Full Gospel church in East Texas, and one of the members was a man 40-some years old who had never walked one step in his life.

I laid hands on him, and I knew the power of God went into him. After praying for him, I went on laying hands on some others. Some of the men got him up, stood him up, turned him loose, and he fell in a heap on the floor. He didn't seem to be any better. That was Monday night.

They carried him into the service Tuesday night — and carried him out. But Wednesday night he came back walking!

The pastor asked him to testify. The platform had a little banister that would have blocked the congregation's view of his feet, so the pastor said, "Brother, get up here on the altar and walk across it (it was a high, wide altar), where everybody can see you."

He got up there and walked across as good as you or I could walk. The pastor had him walk down one aisle and up the other. Then he had him testify.

His testimony was that although he couldn't walk and had never walked in his life, he knew the power of God had been ministered to him. He said, "I went to sleep saying, 'God's healing power is working in me. (That's what we mean by the phrase, "Keep the switch of faith turned on.") It was ministered to me tonight when hands were laid on me. It's working in me to heal me.'

"The first thing I said the next morning when I woke up, still bedfast, was, 'The healing power of God is working in me.' And I kept saying that."

And on Wednesday night he got up and walked. I saw him run up the high steps outside that old church. Just the day before he was a man who had never walked a step in his 40-some years, but that day he was running up the steps and into the church. Glory to God.!

What if he hadn't kept the switch of faith turned on? What if he had said, "Well, they laid hands on me, but it didn't work"? That's not faith, is it? No, that's unbelief.

Keep the switch of faith turned on for the things you are believing God for.

Make this confession:

"My faith in God works! I don't have to depend on someone else to believe God for me. In Christ, I have overcome the devil. In Christ, I can stand in the Father's Presence as though I had never committed a sin. With Christ, I am a joint-heir to all of Heaven's blessings and provisions. No one has a better right to use the Name of Jesus than I do. When I exercise my faith in God, according to His Word, I receive the results His Word promises. My faith in God works!"

ing about the devil and all of his cohorts.

Notice he did not say we are *going* to overcome them; he said we *have* overcome them. How could we have overcome these demons? Because what Christ did was marked to our credit. He did it as our Substitute. (He did it in my place, and God marked it to my credit as though I were the one who did it!)

Someone might argue, "If that's so. . . ."

But if it isn't so, that scripture is a lie.

And if there is one lie in the Bible, then the whole Bible is a lie.

And if the whole Bible is a lie, then there is no God.

And if there is no God, then the Lord Jesus Christ is not Lord; He's not the Son of God; He's a fake.

And if Jesus is not Lord, then there is neither Heaven nor hell.

If all this were so, how dark and hopeless the grave, and what an empty bubble life is!

But friends, the Word of God *is* true. Jesus *is* the Son of God. There *is* a Heaven to gain and a hell to shun. And that verse is not a lie; it's a fact: *"Ye are of God, little children, and have overcome them . . ."* (1 John 4:4).

"Well," somebody will ask, "if we've overcome them, why are we having such a problem with them?"

Because we don't *know* we have overcome them. We don't know what the Bible says about it. When you know what the Bible says, you don't need somebody else to exercise his faith for you; when the devil comes around, you can just laugh at him.

I can understand the problems people have in this area, however. I can relate to people. I've stood where they are. At one time I didn't know this either. I hadn't been taught. And I was afraid of the devil.

If the devil showed up anywhere, I ducked out of the way, trying to hide. I had heard preachers tell how *powerful* the devil is — what all he was going to do — and I didn't want to meet him! If he stuck his head up anywhere, I darted out of the way and hid.

Why? Wasn't I saved? Yes, I was saved. Wasn't I filled with the Holy Spirit?

Yes, I was filled with the Holy Spirit.

I just didn't know the truth.

I'd nearly quake in my boots when the least little thing — opposition or anything — would rise up.

But one day many, many years ago, I found out the truth from the Word of God. When I found out the truth, instead of hoping the devil wouldn't show up, *I went out looking for him!*

I said, "Where is he? I want to meet him. I'm out looking for him. I'm going to laugh at him — that's what I'm going to do! I've already defeated him in Jesus."

I was no longer afraid of the devil. Instead of my darting down a back alley when I saw him coming, now *he* turned and ran when he saw *me* coming. He said, "Oh-oh. He's found out the truth, boys. He's found out the truth. We can't defeat or devour him anymore. He's learned it. He's found out."

If you just *think* you have learned the truth, he'll put you to the test to see if you really believe what you said you believe.

Now can you understand why John

said, "You have overcome them . . ." (1 John 4:4)? You *have* overcome them. Christ acted in your stead. He did it for *you*. You have overcome them because Jesus has overcome them (all these spirits).

Glory to God, you *have* overcome them. You're not *going to* overcome them; you *have* overcome them.

No, we're not bragging about what you are in the flesh. (You don't amount to much in the flesh.) We're talking about who you are *in Christ*.

You can say, *"In Christ*, I conquered Satan. I stripped him of his authority. *And when Jesus arose from the dead, I arose with Him!"* The Bible says that in Ephesians 2.

EPHESIANS 2:1-7
1 And you hath he quickened [or made alive], **who were dead in trespasses and sins;**
2 Wherein in time past ye walked according to the course of this world, according to the prince of the power of the air, the spirit that now worketh in the children of disobedience:
3 Among whom also we all had our conversation [conduct, or manner of life] **in times past**

in the lusts of our flesh, fulfilling the desires
of the flesh and of the mind; and were by
nature the children of wrath, even as others.
4   But God, who is rich in mercy, for his
great love wherewith he loved us,
5   Even when we were dead in sins, hath
quickened us together with Christ, (by grace
ye are saved;)
6   And hath raised us up together, and made
us sit together in heavenly places in Christ
Jesus:
7   That in the ages to come he might shew
the exceeding riches of his grace in his kindness toward us through Christ Jesus.

In the mind of God, we were raised up
with Christ. No wonder John said we have
overcome the enemy. We can make this
passage in Ephesians 2 personal, saying
confidently, "But God, being rich in mercy
with His great love wherewith He loved
me, even when I was dead through my trespasses and sins, made me alive together
with Christ. By grace have I been saved (or
healed). And He raised me up with Him
and made me to sit with Him in the heav-
enlies in Christ."

Just look at verse 7: He's going to put

on a show in the ages to come!

I remember a little old Pentecostal woman years ago down in Texas, bless her heart. The neighbors always gave her trouble because she was a Pentecostal. (They used to call Pentecostals tongue-talkers and Holy Rollers. Pentecostal people were despitefully used.)

One day this woman started to church all dressed up. She had her hat on — women just weren't dressed up in those days if they didn't have a hat on.

One of the neighbor ladies met her as she was walking down the sidewalk and said, "Well, where are you going now? I guess you're going to that church."

The Pentecostal lady had just been reading Ephesians 2 in the Bible, and she said, "No, I'm going to the *show*."

"Oh," she said. "I didn't know you people believed in going to shows." (Pentecostals were Holiness people. They believed in separation from the world.)

"Oh, yes," she said, "we believe in going to the show. God's going to put on a show that's going to last through the ages!"

And that old woman was right, bless God. Looking again at verse 7: *"That in the ages to come he might SHEW the exceeding riches of his grace in his kindness toward us through Christ Jesus."*

He's going to put it on display all through the ages for the devil and his cohorts to see.

Dear friend, it is when you take your place and begin to assume your rights and privileges that God begins to respond to you.

You see, you have the same eternal life Jesus has. The Bible says, *"He that hath the Son hath life . . ."* (1 John 5:12). You have the Son, so you have the life.

That means you can say, "I have taken Jesus as my Savior. I have confessed Him as my Lord. God has given me eternal life — His own nature. I am a new creature, created in Christ Jesus. I have God's ability to perform the good works that were prepared beforehand for me to walk in" (Eph. 2:10).

When you say that, you are just saying what the Scripture says. (I just para-

phrased it for you.) You can say, "I have
God's ability, because I have God's nature.
I have dwelling in me the same great,
mighty, wonderful Spirit that raised Jesus
from the dead."

We can say, quoting First John 4:4,
"Greater is He who is in me than he who is
in the world."

These truths have never registered in
our heart yet. They are Bible facts that
will build faith in you and help you grow to
where *you* can believe God on your own
and not have to depend on someone else.

*And when you get to the place where
you know your faith in God will work, you
will become dangerous to the devil! You
will make hell afraid of you, and you will
make Heaven glad.*

Until you get to this place, even though
you may be saved and filled with the Holy
Spirit, the devil will have you at a disadvantage. He'll hold high carnival in your
body and dominate your life.

Know the facts of God's Word — what
belongs to you and who you are in Him.

Chapter 4
YOU ARE RIGHTEOUS!

For he hath made him to be sin for us, who knew no sin; that we might be made the righteousness of God in him.

— 2 Corinthians 5:21

This wonderful scripture tells us we have the same righteousness as Jesus. To make it personal, we could paraphrase it to read, "God made Him (Jesus) to be sin on my behalf, that I might become the righteousness of God in Him." You could say, "I have become the righteousness of God in Him. There is, therefore, no condemnation unto me, because I am in Christ."

What does "righteousness" mean? First of all, it means right standing with God. *Nobody has any better standing with God than you do.*

Furthermore, you'll never have any *more* righteousness — you'll never have any *better* standing with God — than you have right now! When you get to Heaven, you'll not be any more righteous than you are in this world.

This subject has been misunderstood in the church world. The Bible plainly states that He who knew no sin was made to be sin for us. Nearly everybody believes that part of the verse. That's easy to believe; we've heard it for years. But that's only half of that verse. Can we rejoice over the last half as we can over the first?

You see, it's always easy to believe something about Jesus: something good, something He did, something in His favor. But it's difficult for you to believe something good about yourself, because you have been programmed negatively. The whole world has been programmed negatively.

But if you do not get your mind renewed with these Bible facts — even though you are born again, filled with the Holy Spirit, and speak with tongues — you will remain a negative person and miss the blessings of God. You'll always be in a battle. You'll walk in defeat and failure.

When you know the Word of God, it

will change you. When you come to know that you are made and have become the righteousness of God in Christ Jesus, you will walk out of the narrow place of theology into the boundless fullness of His grace.

So the first part of that verse is true: *"For he hath made him to be sin for us, who knew no sin . . ."* (2 Cor. 5:21). Why was He made to be sin for us? For what purpose? Look at the last half of that verse: *". . . that we might be made the righteousness of God in him."*

If you really understood that, you couldn't hold onto your chair! (The reason that doesn't register on our spirits is because the mind is the door to the heart or spirit, and our minds have been educated along other lines.)

The righteousness of God — that's who we are! I am the righteousness of God. I can't be any more righteous than that.

Righteousness means right standing with God. You can readily understand that our standing with God is in Christ. He is our standing. Therefore, we couldn't have

any better or any worse standing, because
Christ is the same yesterday, today, and
forever.

*You'll not have any better standing with
God tomorrow than you do today.*

*You'll not have any better standing with
God when you get to Heaven than you do
right now.*

Why? Because Jesus Christ is the same
yesterday, today, and forever (Heb. 13:8).
How long? Forever! *Forever!*

Did you notice it said that He who
knew no sin was made to be sin for us that
we might be made the righteousness of
God in Him? That's *in Christ*. He's my
standing. I am in Him. God sees me in
Him. You can't see me in Him, so you are
acquainted sometimes with my physical
shortcomings, mistakes, faults, and failures. I see them myself.

What I need to do is look at myself the
way the Bible says God looks at me. And I
look a whole lot better in Christ than I do
out of Him. The Bible, in fact, tells me that
I am robed in His righteousness — *His*, not
mine.

Righteousness means more to us than right standing with God. That righteousness gives you and me the privilege of standing in God the Father's Presence as though we had never done anything wrong or committed a sin. That's the way God looks upon us.

Sometimes we look at our past and say, "Oh, I've missed it in so many ways. I'm ashamed of myself. I could have done better. Why didn't I do this, and why didn't I do that?" (We are looking at ourselves out of human eyes.)

How does God look on us? He looks on us as though we had never done anything wrong. Remember, He said, *"I, even I, am he that blotteth out thy transgressions for mine own sake, and will not remember thy sins"* (Isa. 43:25).

If He doesn't remember that you ever did anything wrong, why do you keep remembering it? As long as the devil can keep you thinking of your past failures and mistakes, he can hold you at a disadvantage and keep your faith from working. But if you will hold the Word of God up against the devil and laugh at him, you'll put him on the run every time.

So righteousness gives you the privilege of standing in God the Father's Presence as though you had never committed sin.

You see, you have His nature, because you are His very own child. He's your Father. Once you were born again, you got the nature of the Father in your spirit (because He is the Father of spirits). You were born again.

Learn to let His nature in your spirit dominate you. Oh, I know you've got a different nature in the flesh, but you are not supposed to let your body dominate you.